Confessions of an Uncle Tom

. . . I Toil

By
James | Brown

Grio' Publishing, Inc. Alexandria, VA

Copyright © 2010 Grio' Foundation and TWTGroup LLC.
All rights are reserved. Nothing may be reprinted without written consent of the author. This applies to all materials herein presented, except those indicated by publisher credits.

Printed in the United States of America by:

Grio' Foundation
PO Box 4063
Alexandria, VA 22303

Grio' is rooted in the African term griot the storyteller, recorder and keeper of community history and culture.

The Copyright Right Office of The United States of America has registered this work TXu1-574-918.

ISBN-13: 978-0-9845240-0-6
ISBN-10: 0-9845240-0-2

Design and Editing by Gaea L. Honeycutt
Cover Art by Charles Hooks, Jr.
http://www.hooksvisualcommunications.com

For information regarding special discounts for bulk purchases, please contact Grio Special Sales at Amazon.com.

To a new generation of would be Uncle Tom s

Acknowledgements

Thank You Family & Friends!

To our friends and family, especially Mike and Chris who got this thing started over 20 years ago. To Arica, and Joanne, for love and hope. And Tamara, for loving and supporting me through this. Thank you, thank you, thank you for your patience and your love.

To our editor Gaea Honeycutt, I owe you a debt of gratitude beyond words. Thank you for your skill, support and friendship.

To Jimmy. To our sister and brothers Angela, Sherwood and Gary, and friend Yvette Carter, for your invaluable critiques. And to Gary and John, my friends and #1 neegroes!

Most of all, thank you to our parents M? and H? for etching an acute sense of humor into our DNA.

On this journey, we have been truly blessed by the grace of God,
faith, family and friends

Love You All!

Preface: The Story of Uncle Tom

The story of Uncle Tom

The story of Uncle Tom begins with Harriet Beecher Stowe s novel Uncle Tom s Cabin; or Life Among the Lowly, published in 1852 . . . or does it? One night, at a meeting of the Chicago chapter of the Black Panther Party, regarding Martin Luther King, Jr. s latest meeting with Vice President Richard Nixon and Bobby Seale: We ve got to do something about that Uncle Tom m/f. Let s mount a campaign to discredit this m/f because he sure don t speak for us, the real people.

And so, the story begins . . . or does it? Harold, mulatto son of Furness Jones, is the newly appointed butler of Utopia Plantation. When it comes to his attention about the planned escape of several field darkies , he alerts Master Furness. Now the story begins . . . or does it? How does a story ever begin that never ends?

Yet the question remains . . . how did Stowe s hero, an individual seemingly so noble and ideal, come to represent perhaps the most demeaning insult one African American can call another? And how might any sense of humor possibly be seen in such an accusation?

Who decides who is an Uncle Tom? For African American members of the baby boomer generation, perhaps no derogatory term evokes more anxiety or generates more anger than that of Uncle Tom. These two words have come to define the most negative of characteristics that can be attributed to members of the Black community by their own kind.

White America does not suggest, let alone dictate, whom Black Americans consider a Tom . It is perhaps this very empowerment that may be the reason why the term holds such significance in our community.

While Harriet Beecher Stowe s 1852 novel had the intent of making its primary character a heroic figure in presenting to a white audience the evils of slavery, it has been the African American who has redefined and altered the concept of Uncle Tom as the result of social, political and economic realities faced by the group as a whole.

But, who wouldn t want to be White? This is a time when we are the oppressed; the minority in a world where we are one of the majority. Yet, we are on the lowest economic rung of the ladder, have the highest infant mortality rate, reach only the lowest education standards, have the highest unemployment rates, and are most likely to end up in jail. And, to hear them tell it, it s a wonder we even made it out of the worst forms of slavery and racism in earth s history. But, we did

Anyway, maybe it got started by someone with an angst to grind, someone looking to cover one s own behine? It was during the tumult of the 1960s when we saw a focus upon the term Tom as a measurement of one's political or social standing within the ranks of the Black community. Indeed, the very use of the word often defined how one might be evaluated or judged even to the extent of determining one's "blackness" in the eyes of others.

During the 60s, the Black Panther Party and the Nation of Islam were especially associated with the use of the "Tom" terminology in their effort to discredit political and ideological foes. Perhaps more than anyone, these two groups challenged the very virtues that had made Stowe's hero representative of Christian ideal and virtue.

Both groups directed their attacks towards those they perceived as members of the "bourgeoisie" Black middle class leadership. The very essence of Old Tom's character became the means by which the behavior of fellow African Americans could be taken to task for their effort during the Civil Rights struggles of that period.

Which elements of the old slave's character were subjected to ridicule by those seen during the struggle as "militants"? The strong spiritual nature of the African American, however, makes any attack upon the virtues of Christianity extremely difficult to say the least. In Stowe's novel, Uncle Tom strives to become a better Christian and his vision of Christianity is like that of Christ.

As a slave, he recognizes the injustices that are being inflicted on Blacks but his belief in the Bible prevents him from rebelling against the evils of the system. The "militants," to paint a negative image of a Black man, often used these beliefs in connection with his character traits.

You decide who. While Stowe's hero remains forever a fixed caricature in her novel, the criteria for what comprises an Uncle Tom has evolved to some extent within the Black community. Thus, the "Toms" of the 1900's do not fit the same bill as do those deemed to be such at the beginning of a new millennium.

Nevertheless, as with so many of the aspects of the Black experience, its members have found ways to see an element of humor even in defining who or what comprises being an "Uncle Tom". This combination of humor and sarcasm is one of the few situations where African Americans clearly determine the status of members within the group.

As we hope this work illustrates, it is perhaps this keen ability of our people to adapt and find solace in humor that has sustained us during what have been, historically, the most difficult and demanding of situations.

Table of Contents

Acknowledgements 4

Preface: The Story of Uncle Tom 5

Reflections of...me? 11

Check Yourself. 43

44

Think? 49

Act! 67

Know. 118

The Final Score 138

Appendix (General References) I 140

Appendix (Poets) II 144

Appendix (Pictures) III 146

About the Authors 152

Reflections of...me?

UNCLE TOM'S CABIN.

BY

HARRIET BEECHER STOWE.

WITH

Twenty-seven Illustrations on Wood

BY

GEORGE CRUIKSHANK, ESQ.

EVA AND TOPSY.

LONDON:
JOHN CASSELL, LUDGATE HILL.

1852.

Confessions of an Uncle Tom . . . I Toil

2

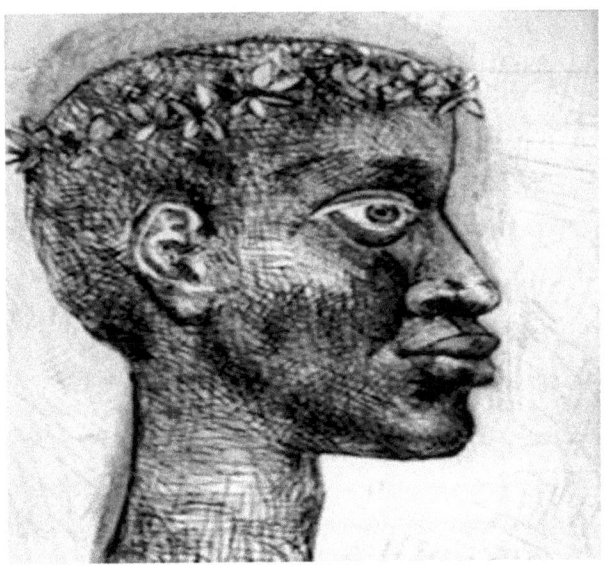

3

Reflections of . . . me

4

Illustration from the Original Edition of Uncle Tom's Cabin

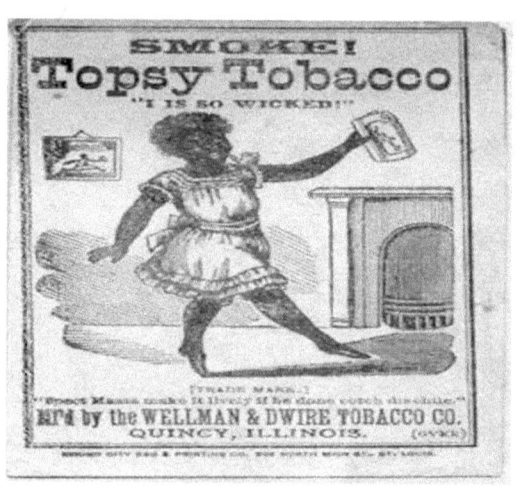

6

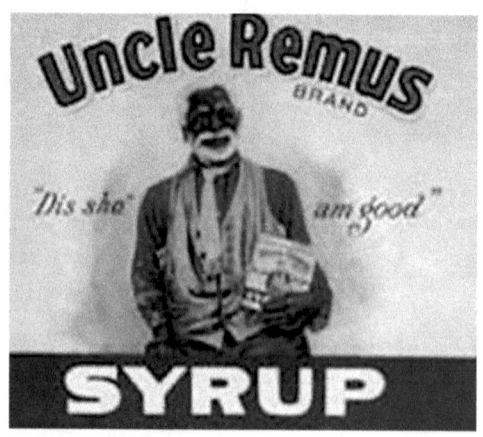

16

Confessions of an Uncle Tom ... I Toil

Confessions of an Uncle Tom . . . I Toil

12

Reflections of . . . me

13

14

Confessions of an Uncle Tom . . . I Toil

15

16

17

18

19

20

21

22

23

24

25

26

27

28

29

30

31

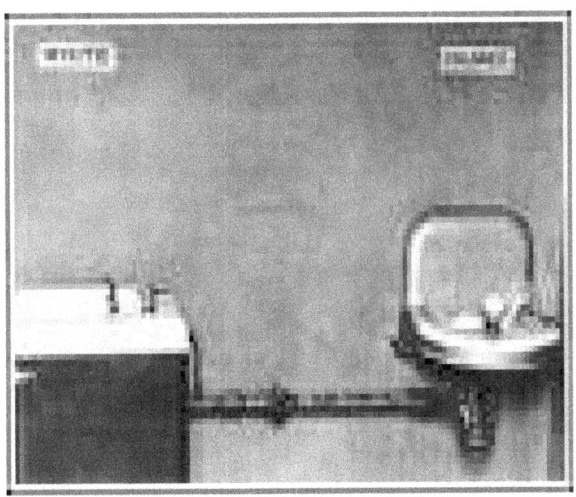

32

33

34

35

36

37

38

39

40

41

Reflections of . . . me

42

43

44

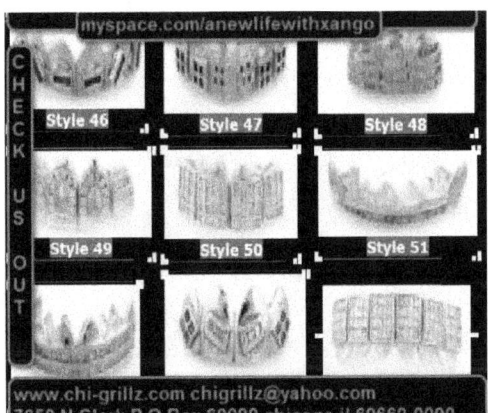

45

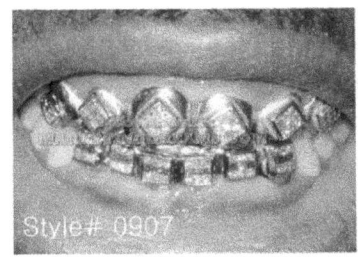

46

Reflections of . . . me

47

48

49

Confessions of an Uncle Tom . . . I Toil

50

51

52

Reflections of . . . me

53

54

55

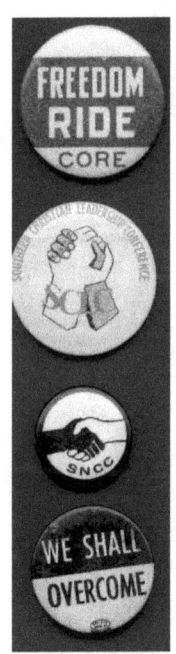

56

57

58

59

60

BLACK ENTERPRISE

TITANS
OF THE B.E. 100s

Black CEOs Who Redefined
and Conquered American Business

DEREK T. DINGLE
Foreword by EARL G. GRAVES

61

62

63

64

65

WEDNESDAY, NOVEMBER 5, 2008

Los Angeles Times

IT'S OBAMA
DECISIVE VICTORY MAKES HISTORY

In California, gay-marriage ban takes early lead

The first black president-elect wins a solid mandate and a fortified Democratic majority in Congress.

NEWS ANALYSIS

Now it's idealism versus realism

Nation watches as state weighs ban

Prop. 8 battle drew money and attention from across the U.S.

PROPOSITION 8
Bans on same-sex marriage
52.5%   47.5%

ELECTORAL VOTES
349   144   45

111TH CONGRESS
The House of Representatives
242   160   33

The Senate
56*   40   4

Analysis: Erasing race assumptions
Roundup of state propositions

Where hope has wrestled with fear

SANDY BANKS

Check Yourself.

Take the Test and Check Yourself

This work is presented in a series of poems and questions, each of which could generate a dissertation. Our intent, however, is to provide a glimpse and let you paint the picture. Over the past 20 years, Donald and I have discussed, posed questions and cajoled individuals into telling us what they think.

The scores assigned are based on the number of people out of 10 who feel that such a response indicates that the respondent is an Uncle Tom. For example: if your response to Stupid Nigger is she should keep quiet and keep her friends (7), then 7 of 10 people surveyed (70%) felt that such a response means the respondent is an Uncle Tom or Tomisine.

So, what s your point basically gives us a chance to solicit your opinion. Also, it can be your cumulative score. Keep a running total so you know, as you should always know in life, where you stand.

Now, let us begin, friend. Let s dis-cover your story s true end!

Please note: These surveys have no real scientific validity. The surveys were conducted informally and primarily with African American sample audiences.

An American, a Negro . . . two souls, two thoughts, two unreconciled strivings; two warring ideals in one dark body, whose dogged strength alone keeps it from being torn asunder.

    W.E.B. Du Bois - The Soul of Black Folk
                                (1901)

Last Question?

Are You an Uncle Tom?

How to answer such a question
       by looking at one s action,
       by looking at one s belief?

       Perhaps by comparing one s to other s
       who have borne the scars,
       suffered the grief?

And who decides who is an Uncle Tom
       someone with an angst to grind,
       someone seeking cover to one s own behine?

       Some say, in the beholder s eye lies
       beauty, and perceptions, are
       often confused with reality?

Are you an Uncle Tom?
       You be the judge and
       judged not. Not by
       your peers, but by . . .

       me

Question #84 — Which is worse?

Q. What is a Black Uncle Tom called?
A. Oreo! Because he is black on the outside, but white on the inside! (2)

Q. What is an Indian Uncle Tom called?
A. Red Apple! Because he is red on the outside, but white on the inside! (3)

Q. What do you call a Latino Uncle Tom?
A. Taco Rubio! Because the wanna be is hard on the outside, but ground round in the middle! (3)

Q. What is an Asian Uncle Tom called?
A. Banana! Because he is yellow on the outside, but white on the inside! (5)

Q. What is a white Uncle Tom called?
A. Benedict Arnold! Because he is your friend on the outside, but a deceiver through and through! (4)

So, what s your point:

Think?

I Thought I was the Chosen One!

I was always special. Tops in my class, I went to a white male college, and then on to graduate school where a major pharmaceutical company recruited me. I was the first Black employee in the company s most prestigious department. One day, we were assembled in the President s conference room to discuss a very important new project when it happened. Jim walked in. A super-star straight out of Harvard B-school. My resentment was palpable and rancid. I was no longer the only one. Jim could see the resentment in my eyes. My body language screamed disdain, intrusion. How dare you! I m the chosen one, the golden child. Jim s sheepish smile simply said, Tom!

me

Think?

Question #83

When another shatters your "exclusive" world, what do you do?

   a. Get downright upset, I thought they loved me? (8)
   b. Feel ashamed of myself? (3)
   c. Dream, Right-on, it's about time, I'm tired of being the token, left on the shelf, displayed for the neighborhood and little else? (2)
   d. Become a mentor, even though Jim, probably, would not want one. Anyway, not you? (1)

OK, what's your point:

Black Bourgeoisie,

    has a gold tooth, sits long hours
    on a stool thinking about money
    sees white skin in a secret room
    rummages his sense for sense
    dreams about Lincoln(s)
    conks his daughter s hair
    sends his coon to school
    works very hard
    grins politely in restaurants
    has a good word to say
    never says it
    does not hate ofays
    hates, instead himself
    him black self

Imamu Amiri Baraka

Question #82

You say that your church, mosque, temple is for everyone, but . . .

    a. Only my kind need attend. (7)
    b. I m not keen bout po people joining. (5)
    c. Poor people can come but please don t sit, at least not next to me! (6)
    d. They re just up in here trying to get what s me and mine, like my daughter! (6)
    e. I do feel special when white people visit! (9)

Yeah, what s your point:

Question #81

Tom belongs to certain religious denominations . . . *

    a. Hebrew (6)
    b. Baptist (4)
    c. LDS   Mormons (7)
    d. Reverend Sun Moon (6)
    e. Purely Spiritual (3)
    f. Muslim   Rawafida (6)
    g. Episcopalian (7)
    h. Catholic (6)
    i. Scientology (7)
    j. Black Muslims (2)
    k. Protestant (3)
    l. Atheist (6)

So, what s your point:

Question #80

You put only $1 in the collection plate because . . .

    a. What they doing for me? (8)
    b. The reverend's probably stealing anyway. (7)
    c. Hey, that's a lot of money! (6)
    d. That's what I always put in. (4)
    e. That's all I got and that's plenty! (2)

Well, what's your point:

Question #79

Even though our forbearers went to all-Black, sometimes one-room shacks, you believe your kids won't get a good education in public schools because . . .

    a. They inherently provide a sub-par education when compared to private schools. (7)
    b. They are for poor people! (9)
    c. They're ok, if you can't get in private school! (6)
    d. They are good if they are in the suburbs. (7)
    e. It's the school's responsibility, not mine or my child's. (8)

So, what's your point:

Question #78

You think one is an Uncle Tom if he. . .

   a. Goes to a white college. (4)
   b. Attends a traditional black elite schools-- Howard, Hampton, Spelman, Morehouse. (2)
   c. Joins the military and worked for the man. (5)
   d. Joins the FBI, CIA, Secret Service, NSA! (7)

And, what s your point:

Question #77

You're still trying to get into the local country club because . . .

   a. Good golf! (4)
   b. To make contacts. (3)
   c. Want to be the first! (8)
   d. My friends go there! (6)

Hey, what s your point:

Question #76 - "The In-Crowd"

In which of these organizations are you or any member of your family a card-carrying member???

    a. Young Republicans (6)
    b. The Moral Majority (8)
    c. Non-Black Greek organization (6)
    d. Black Greek organization (3)
    e. National Rifle Association (8)
    f. Masons (2)
    g. Knights of the Klu Klux Klan (9)
    h. Knights of Columbus (5)
    i. Jaycees (6)
    j. Groove Phi Groove (1)
    k. Fraternal Order of Police (6)
    l. The Moles (3)
    m. Democratic Party (4)
    n. Christian Coalition (5)

Now, what s your point:

The Hood

Living in a hood, struggling every day,
searching for some hope, no one to show the way
what pain do I hide, when I claim to reside
where I don t really stay?

Heathsville, Harlem, white-city,
Africa, my native land or the Hills of Beverly
You know I m from down-south, my nappy roots shout,
back-home, round-the- way!

Truth is, no matter from where I be
I toil to be just
and proud of . . .

me

Question #75

You . . .

   a. Live in Harlem but tell everyone that you live in Manhattan! (8)
   b. Live in Roxbury but say Boston. (7)
   c. Live in Compton but tell everyone L.A. (7)
   d. Live in North Philly but tell everyone West Mt. Airy. (7)
   e. Grew up in someplace like Ardmore, but front like you're from someplace like North Philly. (7)
   f. Are proud to be a hood rat? (3)

Sure, what's your point:

The new neighbors . . .

I live in a new   hood ,
though I tell people otherwise
where people still yell nigger
as they drive by.

But, still I get upset when other negroes move in, my
 new   nice mixed neighborhood filled, still
with lawn jockeys
and lantern men.

me

Question #74

When the "new" negro, black, African American family moves into your nice mixed neighborhood, you assume that they . . .

   a. Are going to mess it up. (7)
   b. Will be parking on the lawn. (7)
   c. Won t know how to act. (6)
   d. Finally, I won t be the pioneer anymore. (2)
   e. Will be country. (6)
   f. Can t afford to live here. (5)
   g. Must be up to no good. (8)

Well, what s your point:

Question #73

Do you believe that prejudice is worse?

   a. In the South (6)
   b. North (5)
   c. Texas (4)
   d. Canada (3)
   e. South Africa (4)
   f. Sweden (4)
   g. Australia (3)
   h. France (4)
   i. Cuba (5)
   j. Brazil (5)
   k. Egypt (3)

And, what s your point:

Question #72

You believe that white people . . .

   a. Don t live in ghettoes. (6)
   b. Aren t on welfare. (7)
   c. Are basically just like me. (3)
   d. Have happier family lives. (6)
   e. Commit fewer crimes. (6)
   f. Know their history/culture. (7)
   g. Are all rich! (8)

Well, what s your point:

Question #71

You feel (just a little) honored . . .

   a. To have white people wait on you! (8)
   b. To have a white bus driver on your route. (6)
   c. To work in white neighborhoods? (6)
   d. To give extra special attention to the white customers in your line! (5)

And, what s your point:

Question #70

The Uncle Tom sees little to no fault in his oppressor, because . . . *

    a. He believes that he is responsible for his oppression. (2)
    b. His master or oppressor is responsible for his happiness! (9)
    c. The bible sanctions it! (7)

So, what s your point:

Question #69

Favorite Eatin' Places: Which of these fine dining establishments do you frequent?

    a. Denny s (7)
    b. Sambo s (9)
    c. Mickey D s (2)
    d. KFC (2)
    e. Cracker Barrel (4)
    f. Woolworth s (3)
    g. Chi Chi s (5)
    h. Bojangles (3)
    i. Sylvia s (1)
    j. Gates & Sons (1)

Well, what s your point:

Question #68

Do you buy . . .

    a. White eggs because they are better than brown eggs? (5)
    b. White rice because it is better than brown? (6)
    c. Light bread because it tastes better than wheat? (5)
    d. Karo because it is better than black molasses! (6)

So, what s your point:

Question #67

Are you still uncomfortable taking a seat at the lunch counter?

    a. Naw, naw, hell naw! (0)
    b. True, true, too true!!! (10)

Hey, what s your point:

Question #66

Avoid these foods at the company picnic?

    a. Watermelon (6)
    b. Fried chicken (4)
    c. Ribs (9)
    d. Totally offended if offered any of that stuff, especially, chitterlings! (5)

So, what s your point:

Question #65

Hesitant to order ethnic food when out?

    a. Never, never with strangers! (6)
    b. Never, never with my white friends. (8)
    c. I don't eat ethnic foods. (7)
    d. Why the (#@&!) not . . . it's all ethnic food. (2)

Well, what's your point:

Question #64

Uncle Tom's Menu! Let's consider your preferences — especially when eating around other people.

Menu 1	Points	Menu 2	Points
Baked Chicken		Fried Chicken	
Rack-o-lamb		Bar-b-que Ribs	
Sweet Peas		Black-eyed Peas	
Cantaloupe		Watermelon	
Carrot Cake		Pound Cake	
Pretzels		Potato Chips	
Tripe		Chitlins	
Spinach		Collard Greens	
Fish Cake		Crab Cake	
Salmon		Fried Whiting	
Bouillabaisse		Gumbo	
Pancake		ho Cake	
Iced Coffee		Kool-Aid	
Lamb Chops		Pork Chops	
Linguine		Macaroni & Cheese	
Mashed Potatoes		Candied Yams	
Mussels		Fried Oysters	
Beef Stew		Oxtail Soup	
Pepsi		Coke	
Pumpkin Pie		Sweet Potato Pie	
Pasta & Sauce		Rice & Gravy	
Asparagus		String Beans	
Total			

Subtract total on right from left for your overall score. For example, if you total 12 on the right and 10 on the left, then 10 - 12 = -2. You may be less of a Tom than you thought. What s your point?

The Scoring Process . . .

The scores assigned are based on the number of people out of ten who feel that such a response indicates that the respondent is an Uncle Tom. For example: if your response to Question #63 is [c]   she should keep quiet and keep her friends (7)   then 7 out 10 people surveyed (70%) feel that such a response means you are an Uncle Tom or Tomisine.

What s your score . . . brother . . . sister?

Think: The Score
Check Yourself

The Score	Overall Range
Soul Brother/Sister #1	0 75
Uncle Tom Tendencies	76 125
Borderline Uncle Tom	126 200
Closet Uncle Tom	201 300
YOUR SCORE	

Act!

"Stupid nigger!"

"I thought, they were my best friends."

We were one of two black families in this ritzy enclave of private schools and swimming pools.

Returning from a night of righteous partying in New York, we were having fun . . . the Mercedes hummed and the doobies glowed as Grover urged, Let it flow! Some of the nicest girls at school . . . and now I was one of them . . . I loved them.

At the turnpike exit, an ordinary toll-booth attendant almost mistakenly returned too much change. Stupid nigger! . . . they laughed (I choked) til tears filled their eyes . . . (I cried). Oops, sorry Sera, but you re not like them anyway, you re different.

In that moment of blind silence my heart fell like a rock upon a deep cold pond . . . they didn t mean any harm, I thought, they were my best friends.

me

Question #63

You think . . .

    a. They didn t mean any harm, they just don t know any better. (8)
    b. Later for these fools, it s time for some new friends. (2)
    c. Remain quiet, don t betray their trust, and keep her friends. (7)
    d. Tell em. Tell em now before it gets out of hand. (3)

Now, what s your point:

Only we are a problem?

I have always, from time to time, thought I was a problem.

In high school, I was part of the minorities ,
living in our own little section of town,
 white city ,
In college, I was one of the TYP
(transitional year program) students, not
because they were smarter, just
because we were who we were and
they needed federal funds.
At work, I was an affirmative action hire, not
because they worked harder, just
because we were who we were and
they wanted tax breaks.
Now they say
I am an illegitimate, illiterate, a felon not
because they are any more virtuous, just
because they are who they are and they
need to have a problem.

me

Question #62

You think, we are the problem, because . . .

    a. It is on the morning, evening and nightly news . . . so it must be true? (8)
    b. This is part of a conspiracy of ignorance? (5)
    c. We are just too sensitive and blind to the facts? (7)
    d. We are our own worst enemies? (3)
    e. It s their problem, not mine? (2)

Well, what s your point:

What are you?

Am I colored or Black, yesterday s negro or today s African American?

My mother is part Indian, my great grandfather, part German or Jew, and I am from down south. But my father s father s people come from the islands, I think. And my mama, her father was real light.

They say they come from old man Wagner s plantation. They were Irish, I think.

Well, ultimately, I know we must go all the way back to African royalty, right?

When I was little, my friends teased me about being a nigger. A black one at that. It hurt my feelings to be called coffee black cause when I looked in the mirror, I saw Superman, or better yet, Clark Kent. And I just can t be all nigga cause surely you can see, that with this wavy hair and sharp nose, I got Indian in me . . . I toil . . .

me

Question #61

When it comes to race, you are quick to note . . .

   a. I got Indian in me. (8)
   b. Girl, you got that good hair. (8)
   c. If you light, you all-right. If you brown, stick around. But if you black, GET BACK! (9)
   d. Damn . . . all that yella, wasted on that ugly fella. (8)
   e. Did your mama say your girlfriend would have to pass the paper bag test? (9)
   f. Whatever happened to Say it loud . . . ? (1)

And, what s your point:

. . . I toil.

Question #60

I think, I don't know, what I am . . .

   a. Part white (7)
   b. Part Indian (8)
   c. African-American (3)
   d. Negro (5)
   e. Black, just not all Black! (4)

Now, what s your point:

To A Dark Girl

I love you for your brownness
And the rounded darkness of your breast.
I love you for the breaking sadness in your voice
And shadows where your wayward eye-lids rest.

Something of old forgotten queens
Lurks in the lithe abandon of your walk
And something of the shackled slave
Sobs in the rhythm of your talk.

Oh, little brown girl, born for sorrow s mate,
Keep all you have of queenliness,
Forgetting that you once were slave,
And let your full lips laugh at Fate!

*Gwendolyn B.
Bennett*

Question #59

Do your thick lips and broad nose make you feel and look . . .

    a. Like an African? (1)
    b. Full of juice? (4)
    c. Like a monkey? (7)
    d. Lower class? (9)
    e. Like Bozo the clown? (6)
    f. Hey stuff? (2)

Question #58

Can you really engage in bleaching and other forms of "cosmetic" surgery and truly love yourself? Who would you ask for advice?

    a. Michael Jackson (8)
    b. Mariah Carey (7)
    c. Malcolm Little (1)
    d. RuPaul (6)
    e. Latoya Jackson (9)
    f. Dick Clark (5)
    g. Dennis Rodman (4)

Now, what's your point:

Question #57

Who really decides whether or not you are beautiful?

a. The fashion industry! Look for the label . . . Polo, Hilfiger, Willie Wear, Colours, Fubu, Versace, et al. (8)
b. Nobody. Just me! I set my own style. (3)
c. Only white people are truly beautiful . . . they set the standard. (6)
d. I invent my own style. Fashion is for those who need someone to tell them what to wear. (1)

So, what s your point:

Question #56

"Girl! You got that good hair!" What is good hair?

a. Naturally nappy (3)
b. Bald (4)
c. Braided (3)
d. Afro (2)
e. Dreadlocks (2)
f. Weave (7)
g. Wavy (5)
h. Conked (9)
i. No such thing (1)

And, what s your point:

Question #55

Which of these items are parts of your hair care?

    a. Do rag (7)
    b. Straightening comb (6)
    c. Jeri curl juice (9)
    d. Relaxer (7)
    e. Perm kit (8)
    f. Weave rope? (8)

Hey, what s your point:

Question #54

Got no butt, but proud of it?

    a. Kind of (7)
    b. Totally (8)
    c. What? You sayin I ain t got no behind! (6)
    d. Shit!!! They call me Bertha Butt! (2)

So, what s your point:

Question #53

My my my . . . did or do you?

  a. Wear blue, gray, green, yellow, hazel or any color, contact lens. (8)
  b. Say things like, When I was born I had blue, hazel, green, or gray eyes! (7)
  c. Dye your hair blonde, orange, purple, green, black??? (4)
  d. Sneak a look at the color of your newborn baby's eyes!?! (8)

So, what's your point:

Question #52

Com'on, admit it now, you enjoy being told . . .

  a. You're special . . . (4)
  b. You're different . . . (7)
  c. You're a credit to your race . . . (8)
  d. You're not like those other ones . . . (7)

Hey, what's your point:

Question #51

You expect that African Americans are . . .

    a. Not naturally daring. (6)
    b. Unenterprising. (7)
    c. Lazy. (8)
    d. Shiftless. (9)
    e. Invisible. (2)
    f. Full of the self-hate that holds me back. (3)

Hey, what s your point:

Question #50

You act like these rights are as, if not more, important than Black rights . . .

    a. Gay rights (8)
    b. Women s rights (7)
    c. Right to life (6)
    d. Handicap accessibility (5)

Now, what s your point:

Question #49

You act like you did it on your own and get upset because . . .

a. You are successful and most other blacks are a bunch of lazy niggas. (9)
b. Your success has nothing to do with affirmative action or the Civil Rights Movement. (8)
c. If they just worked harder, they would be rewarded. (7)
d. In the current meritocracy you have as much a chance to win as any of the Mayflower kids. (5)
e. If he gets a chance from a special program, he may bring you down and make you look bad! (6)

Well, what s your point:

Searching for light . . .

I seek the skin my sin soaks in.

Every day I beat the drum
Black is beautiful. Black is beautiful!   We re #1!
Superman by day, me at night
just in every way, just, searching for light.

At night I sneak the streets
it s the pedestal girl I seek.
Like the hero of Tuskegee
club hopping round,
hoping no one sees me
up and down the ho zones I glide
past all night clinics and crack houses I slide
round corners and moaners, girls getting by.

One eye out for the
wee girls of fleeting fame
and one-night stands, the other
for big brother s undercover scam
That one! That one! She s kind of cute
is she white, is she Spanish?
She hops in, then we vanish.
Was she a cop, not
if she feels right here.

Tonight a mate
this date ,
with the would be beautiful leper.
Wander no more
she s alright
maybe a whore
at least she s white.

me

Question #48

You only date light-skinned people because . . .

    a. My parents was light. (6)
    b. Mannnn, I only date dem light-skin girls with dat long hair cause they are fine! (5)
    c. Never. The blacker the berry, the sweeta the juice. (2)
    d. No, cause it really doesn t matter. Can t we all just get some!!! (3)
    e. Sure! First thing they got to do is pass the paper-bag test. Anything darker, no pass. (6)
    f. I remember a time when dark-skin girls were so shameful, jealous and resentful, that they went around in gangs cutting the face of their light-skin sisters just to make them feel ugly too . . . did you? (10)

And, what s your point:

Question #47

Do you talk all Black but long to date white girls on the sly?

    a. No, not me . . . liar! (6)
    b. Only once in awhile. (3)
    c. True, true, too true! (8)
    d. I only date Spanish or Asians . . . on the side. (6)

So, what s your point:

She is not you.

Sometimes I only imagine
anticipating
her taste
rich and creamy, totally free.
We pretend
we are not together

It s like she s just, like me.
Even when out with friends
that seem to understand
they could just pretend.
We sneak to find time
together.

She is not you
in a thousand different ways
you are better
but she is a difference
and satiates my thirst
for variety . . .

me

Question #46

With your interracial date, are you . . .

   a. Ashamed to be seen in public? (8)
   b. Reluctant to hold hands? (5)
   c. Likely to introduce as just friends? (5)
   d. Pretending it s just a business thang ! (6)

Now, what s your point:

Out of Africa?

I love my parents.
We moved from the inner city
before I finished middle school. Fact was
dark-skin girls were cutting faces
of light-skin girls.
They didn t like feeling we were prettier.

My family lived in the City s first projects; part of the 1st
war on urban blight.
My mother was the telephone company s first black
female operator.
She was as brown as night, but, my father was blacker
than black even though he looked white. Needless to say,
I was somewhat light.

Yes, we were apart of urban flight.
Not afraid of Black, afraid for being light.
Sometimes I wonder, will they hate in Africa, too . . .

me

Question #45

You believe . . .

   a. Dark-skin girls should love light-skin and/or white boys only? (9)
   b. Face it, light-skin girls are prettier than dark-skin girls. I don t make the rules; it s just the way it is, here and everywhere. (9)
   c. Some guys are hesitant to date white girls, so light girls are the next best thing. (8)
   d. Light-skin girls think they are better than dark-skin girls. (7)
   e. My friends are all colors. I don t care about the color on the outside, just, the color on the inside. (1)
   f. Is there anything finer than a truly beautiful dark-skin girl? (2)
   g. Africans don t feel there is any difference between light-skin or dark-skin non-African. You re all slaves! (9)

So, what s your point:

Question #44

You act as if Black women . . .

   a. Make the best mammies. (10)
   b. Are just plain old sexy. (3)
   c. Run around promiscuous. (8)
   d. Are a bunch a nappy headed ho s (9)
   e. Know what they want!?! (2)

Hey, what s your point:

Question #43

You have penis envy, because . . .

    a. Only Black men have a large penis. (8)
    b. 80% 90% do. (7)
    c. Less than half do. (4)
    d. Size doesn t matter . . . shitttttt!!!! (3)

Hey, what s your point:

Question #42

When you see a group of young black men together, you think . . .

    a. Thugs. (8)
    b. Gang. (7)
    c. Posse. (7)
    d. Basketball-players. (8)
    e. Just guys. (2)

Hey, what s your point:

Question #41

. . . but, if they are white, you think . . .

a. Club . (8)
b. Friends. (7)
c. Team. (6)
d. Chums! (7)
e. Just the guys. (2)

Well, what s your point:

Question #40

The Uncle Tom is afraid to walk through, live or shop in . . .

a. South Boston. (6)
b. Montana. (7)
c. Alabama. (8)
d. Chicago. (6)
e. Bedford Stuyvesant, Queens. (5)
f. Grays Ferry Philadelphia. (5)

So, what s your point:

Question #39

Litter.
You're walking down the block.
You're riding down the street.
You're taking the bus . . . it doesn't matter!

What do you do with that gum wrapper, soda can, cigarette, half-eaten fruit or whatever piece of trash?

- a. Throw it on the ground, cause they don't have garbage cans in my neighborhood. (6)
- b. Throw it on the ground, but not in nice (white) neighborhoods. (7)
- c. Throw it on the ground, but not in my neighborhood. (7)
- d. Wait until I find a trash can. (1)
- e. And I piss in my alleys, leave garbage out front, write graffiti, and shop in dirty little stores in the neighborhood! (8)

Hey, what's your point:

Notes on a Return to My Native Land

At the end of the small hours: this town, flat, dis-played . . .

And I, and I,
I who sang with clenched fist
You must be told the length to which I carried cowardice.
In a tram one night, facing me, a Negro.
He was a Negro tall as a pongo who tried to make himself
very small on a tram seat. On that filthy tram seat he
tried to abandon his gigantic legs and his starved boxer s
trembling hands. And everything had left him, was
leaving leaving him . . .
. . .
And the whole thing added up perfectly to a hideous
Negro, a peevish Negro, a melancholy Negro, a slumped
Negro, hands folded as in prayer upon a knotty stick.
A Negro shrouded in an old, threadbare jacket. A Negro
who was comical and ugly, and behind me women giggled
as they looked at him.
He was COMICAL AND UGLY.
COMICAL AND UGLY, for a fact.
I sported a great smile of complicity . . .
My cowardice rediscovered!
I bow to the three centuries which support my civil
rights and my minimized blood.
My heroism, what a joke!
This town suits me to perfection . . .

Aimé Césaire

Question #38

Why are you reluctant to shop at black-owned stores?

    a.   They dirty! (7)
    b.   They ain t got the good stuff. (6)
    c.   Ok, if it s a bar, barber or beauty shop or rib crib. (5)
    d.   I would if there was some in my neighborhood. (6)
    e.   Naw, we only shop in white or mixed neighborhoods! (8)
    f.   Who me? I love throwing down with the brothers! (1)
    g.   Naw, naw, hell naw . . . too much attitude! (3)

Now, what s your point:

Question #37

The Uncle Tom only eats and shops in white neighborhoods because . . .

    a.   They get the better stuff. (4)
    b.   The places are cleaner. (5)
    c.   The people are friendlier. (6)
    d.   I can afford it!!!! (5)

Well, what s your point:

Question #36

Do you only go out to the movie in white or mixed neighborhoods because?

    a. People know how to act over there (6)
    b. The place is cleaner (5)
    c. It s safer (4)
    d. They get the good movies (4)
    e. Who me? I love throwing down with the brothers! (1)
    f. There ain t no theaters in my neighborhood!!! (1)

And, what s your point:

Question #35

Are you uncomfortable in certain stores buying certain foods?

    a. Sometimes when I m buying watermelon. (6)
    b. Just a little embarrassed at the check-out counter (5)
    c. Naw man . . . I only go in black neighborhoods for those kinds of things. (4)

So, what s your point:

Question #34

Why don't you patronize black professionals and other contractors?

- a. Well, maybe if they work for a white company. (8)
- b. Can t find black contractors in your neighborhood. (7)
- c. Black contractors are too expensive. (6)
- d. Always have to get the work redone. (7)
- e. Feel they don t have enough experience in the field. (6)
- f. Who me? I love throwing down with the brothers! (1)
- g. My parents and grandparents always said, don t trust em!! (8)

So, what s your point:

The Pilot

Back when I was growing up I dreamed of flying, straight-up above the clouds, out-there anywhere free, to be just me, above the norm soaring to places known and unknown. But, in that day, you had to be smart and trained, neat and pressed, large and in-charge and, white.

Ten years, my own company, two degrees and another ten years later, we were boarding a plane for Senegal with a group of winners of our Black history. The airport was packed, so, while the kids played, we rushed to get gum and something to read and make sure everyone had peed. Despite the normal pre-flight jitters, this was an adventure and we wanted to be prepared. They called our boarding row and as we anxiously entered the cabin, I peeped into the cockpit and discovered, oh no, oh my God, the pilot, she s Black!

me

Question #33

Where do these thoughts still come from? Would you . . .

    a. Make an excuse, any excuse, but get off the plane? (9)
    b. Buckle-up, what the fuck. No pain (hopefully), no gain? (2)
    c. Think, All right now, we've finally made it? (1)
    d. Check to see if at least the co-pilot is white? (7)

Hey, what's your point:

My Home, Africa . . .

I thought, maybe if I could go home,
to Africa, I d find a piece of mine.
Surely, by embracing my true ancestors, I d find,
someone or something to enlighten my mind.

There, I d appreciate that Africa is the birthplace of man,
that place where kings and Pharaohs built magnificent communities
long before the civilization of Europe or Asian lands.
I d see beautiful black people, not African-Senegalese, or
African-Gambians, and definitely not African-Americans,
but Black people.
Poets, scholars and scientists. Pilots from Ethiopia.
And businessmen from the Serif and Wolof tribes.

But something was wrong.
Great markets and shops lined the streets
banks and businesses like IBM titivate the plazas
but they were owned by the Lebanese and French.
Mauritanians and Arabs were quick to declare
that they were not Africans, and definitely not African-Americans.
An Ethiopian pilot pointed out,
sometimes the Senegalese and Cote Ivorians
are more French than the French.

Still Africa was Africa, my ultimate home
though now I appreciate I am an American
no matter where I roam . . . I toil.

me

Question #32

Where are you from? The Uncle Tom doesn't know where, but he "knows" it wasn't from Africa, because . . .

    a. Africa is the jungle and backward. (6)
    b. If we are from Africa, we are descended from royalty. (5)
    c. Africans sold us into slavery. (4)
    d. Being poor here is still better than living there. (6)
    e. I don t know the part of Africa I come from. (2)
    f. They won t like me if I go there! (5)

And, what s your point:

Question #31

True brothers and sisters . . .

    a. Don t talk white! (8)
    b. Are against capital punishment! (6)
    c. Feel all Black people are good! (7)
    d. All think alike! (6)
    e. Only vote Democratic! (5)

So, what s your point:

Question #30

Yet, when you see "true" black people you . . .

    a. Quickly, lock your car doors. (7)
    b. Clutch your pocketbook. (6)
    c. Are afraid of people wearing dashikis and baggy clothes and all that other mess. (6)
    d. Watch em like a hawk while they're in your store. (7)
    e. Assume that their credit card or check is not going to clear. (7)
    f. Serve the white customers first. (9)
    g. Think, If they are in here they must just work here. (6)

Hey, what's your point:

"Sell-out"

Sell-out!
C. Delores may shout
I ain t no bitch, nigga,
mutherfcuker, you the sellout.
 pose to be a brother,
what-ever happened to Public Enemy
they didn t get rich dissin me.
Don t get me wrong, I want nice things too.
But damn, is tomorrow just about cars and jewelry
Or are you just another shill
toiling on a payment plan
Why don t you try dissin the man!
But you can t.
Better just rant,
than end up scant
That be why there be no doubt,
you just another
mutherfcuking sell-out!

me

Question #29

What is a "gangsta" Tom?

a. Talk (rap) about Black people worse than whites ever have! (8)
b. Women are hos . . . naw, naw . . . bitches! (9)
c. Only call em hos, bitches and niggas on the record . . . for the money; but, off the record, they ok! (10)
d. Talking Ebonics with your homeys, but switch to English when whites enter the scene. (8)

Now, what s your point:

"Black Cop Black Cop Black Cops . . . Stop!"

He was one of the first black/colored/negro cops in this town, after having spent nearly twenty years as a military policeman. They gave him the colored side of town. Everyday he saw abuse, robberies, drugs and scams. Some of his own people tried to con him. Then there was the man who always wanted more. He heard, he was like all the rest. To top it off, his own son thought he was a fool. That was cool, it came with the job, just part of wearing the uniform. He knew who he was, but it was getting to him, one day . . .

Blue-black smoke and the smell of burning rubber leapt from the road as screeching tires halt in front of a group of black kids playing hoops. You jump from the car as your partner says, . . . hold on! they re just a bunch of kids.

me

Question #28

You . . .

   a. Say: It s time somebody teaches these good for nothings a lesson! (9)
   b. Think: I m not going to let my boss think I m soft on these hoodlums!?! (8)
   c. Act: Hello fellas, can we ask you a few questions? (4)
   d. Know: Just some brothers playing ball, so: Yo brothers, what s up? (2)

Well, what s your point:

Road Trip

Right on? Right on? Have you ever felt you weren t going to be welcomed when you went in a store? Or that the waitress was taking her time to wait on you because you re Black? How about the feeling you get when you are walking or driving in certain neighborhoods?

It was 1974. We were five young (broke ass) Black guys driving through New Jersey headed down South through the Carolinas, Georgia, Alabama and Mississippi to Houston for our fraternity s national conclave . . . a party! Our stomachs (I know mine was) were tight when we got in the car. We managed to catch our breath in D.C., Atlanta and Tuskegee, but now we had to stop in Mississippi.

We picked a Mickey D s. TC and I went in while Mr. Wonderful, Slick and Low waited in the car. We were hoping for the best, but prepared for the worst. We got our stuff and ran outta there. So fast, in fact, half way down the road, we realized we had forgotten our change.

We have to go back? No, not that. We can t go back. We have to go back! When we walked in, little miss thing started to grin, You forgot your change. Here. Please, come again!

That s when we realized, Hey, they are pretty nice. The road trip to Houston and back was a blast!

Sometime(s), we are our own worst enemy. Right on! Right on!

me

Question #27

You believe . . .

    a. Whew! But, after all, this was a McDonald s. (3)
    b. A passing thought: Maybe they could see that I was different. (8)
    c. These m/f s better have my money. I thought that to myself. (5)
    d. Thank God, it wasn t Denny s! (4)

So, what s your point:

Question #26

    Are you a crab too?

    You know you are an Uncle Tom when your number one pastime is being the crab in the bucket!

    Ever notice how when crabs are in a bucket and one tries to climb out, the other crabs, which should be trying to help in the escape, instead reach up and pull the would be escapee back down in the bucket with the rest of em!

What is that all about!?

    a. Naw, naw, hell naw! (10)
    b. True, true, too true!!! (0)

Now, what s your point:

Question #25

You act like . . .

    a. You ain't use to nothing, so you don't know no better! (4)
    b. That having nothing is better than having something taken away from him/her! (7)
    c. If you can't have it, then nobody can! (8)
    d. It's all about me, not we! (9)
    e. I got mine, too bad if you don't get yours! (9)
    f. Someone's else's loss is the whole world's loss! (2)

Hey, what's your point:

Question #24

You behave like someone who should still instinctively go in the back door of restaurants?

    a. Naw, naw, hell naw! (0)
    b. True, true, too true!!! (10)

Well, what's your point:

Question #23

You behave like someone who should sit in the back of the bus?

    a. Naw, naw, hell naw! (3)
    b. True, true, too true!!! (7)

So, what's your point:

Question #22

You act like someone who should sit in a separate part of the theater?

    a. Naw, naw, hell naw! (4)
    b. True, true, too true!!! (6)

Well, what s your point:

Question #21

You still drink out of the "for coloreds only" water fountain — when you can find one?

    a. Naw, naw, hell naw! (0)
    b. True, true, too true!!! (10)

Hey, what s your point:

Question #20

PC — "politically cracked". You actively campaigned for . . .

    a. Barry Goldwater (9)
    b. Bill Clinton (1)
    c. George Wallace (5)
    d. The second time (4)
    e. McCain/Palin (7)
    f. Alan Keyes (8)

Now, what s your point:

Question #19

The Uncle Tom is an avid supporter of . . .

    a. Clarence Thomas (8)
    b. Shelby Steele (6)
    c. Colin Powell (2)
    d. Al Sharpton (3)
    e. Rush Limbaugh (9)

And, what s your point:

Question #18

Your less than stellar results in school offer the following scant career possibilities: shoe shine boy, lawn jockey, baggage handler, chamber maid, drug dealer or washroom attendant.

    a. Naw, naw, hell naw! (10)
    b. True, true, too true!!! (0)

Well, what s your point:

Question #17

You go by any of these nicknames: dusty, topsie, boy, jack, govnor, doctor.

    a. Naw, naw, hell naw! (10)
    b. True, true, too true!!! (0)

Well, what s your point:

'The Million Dollar Niggas'

Remember Marge Schott, owner of the Cincinnati Reds baseball team who referred to the team s Black ballplayers as her million dollar niggas . Or Bert Campaneris, General Manager of the Los Angeles Dodgers who considered black players incapable of professional sport team ownership or management.

me

Question #16

Your reaction . . .

    a. Probably right given the complexities of team management and ownership. (9)
    b. Blacks are better as athletes than as business people. (7)
    c. We'll be ready soon. (3)
    d. Didn't Blacks manage their own league once-upon-a-time? (2)

Hey, what's your point:

Question #15

Which is your favorite?

Q: What do you call a black man in a tree?
A: A branch manager. (5)

Q: Why doesn't Mexico have an Olympic team?
A: Because everyone who can run, jump and swim is already in the U.S. (5)

Chinese Proverb: When Chinaman commit a crime, get good laugh when description is passed around (black hair, brown eyes, glasses). **(5)**

Q: How many Polaks does it take to change a light bulb?
A: Three. One to stand on a chair and hold the bulb and the other two to spin the chair. (5)

Q: How do you make an Italian?
A: Put a black in one hand, a Jew in the other, and slam them together. WOP!! (5)
(W.O.P. – without papers – once upon a time they were the illegal aliens.)

Q: What's the difference between a pizza and a Jew?
A: Pizzas don't scream when you put them in an oven. (10)

Q: What do you call a black test tube baby?
A: Janitor in a drum. (5)

Question #14

At work or play, which ethnic jokes do you laugh at . . .

    a. I only laugh at the black ones? (8)
    b. I don t laugh! I may giggle, smile or smirk, but I don t laugh! (6)
    c. Who cares, who does it hurt? (7)
    d. Does this mean I can t have a sense of humor? (5)

Now, what s your point:

Question #13

    Black Face   Ben Vereen sang in black face at Bill Clinton s Presidential inauguration. Sammy Davis hugged and kissed all over Richard Nixon at his. Many, many, many considered their behavior stone Uncle Tomish , but . . .

How do you act in similar (don't play! you know what I mean!) situations???

    a. Hey! When in Rome, do as the Romans. (8)
    b. I get blacker than Black! (6)
    c. "I act the same, no matter whose presence I'm in." (2)
    d. Something comes over me . . . I just can t help myself. (7)
    e. I want to be liked, so I act accordingly. (6)

Well, what s your point:

Question #12

Black Jelly Beans   Texaco Oil Company settled a racial discrimination suit resulting from alleged comments made by white senior managers referring to African American employees as the black jelly beans left stuck and unwanted at the bottom of a bag.

Your reaction to these comments:

  a. Was it true or just a joke? (5)
  b. The comments of a misguided few, no trust was broke (cause no trust existed, only history) at least we were trying . . . I toil. (5)
  c. Come on, it s just a joke. What s the big deal? (4)
  d. Maybe so, maybe not. It is the way I feel. (6)
  e. I don t like em (black jelly beans) either. (5)

And, what s your point:

Do it. Just do it.

What the fuck, you son-of-a-bitch mother-fucking bastard cum sucking cock licking flat-ass nose picking chicken shit ofay cracker shit-head limp dick half wit would-be god pecker-wood red-neck know-it-all Bozo the clown looking big nose bad breath fish smelling control freak paranoid asshole of the ages murdering thieving conniving arrogant cunt sucking private-ass-licking Johnny-come-lately non dancing racist sexist pig-shit eating cockroach who thinks every man should worship you just because you you you stereotyping profiling bull-shitting selfish faggot whore rapist corn-holing little dick lazy fuck wanting everyone to do for you bigot nazi skin head mass-murdering genocider spawn of Satan idiotic complaining back biting weasel smelling like a dog and can t jump worth a shit you gun toting hillbilly cracker punk-ass bitch neanderthal slave mongering whiter than the whitest white man black-ass nigger!

(I said that to myself.)

Yes . . . sir?

me

Question #11

You wonder . . .

    a. Did I say that out loud? (3)
    b. Did I act that out loud? (4)
    c. Did she just know? (4)
    d. How long have I (how long can I) kept that bottled up? (5)

Hey, what s your point:

The Scoring Process . . .

The scores assigned are based on the number of people out of ten who feel that such a response indicates that the respondent is an Uncle Tom. For example: if your response to Question #63 is [c]   she should keep quiet and keep her friends (7)   then 7 out 10 people surveyed (70%) feel that such a response means you are an Uncle Tom or Tomisine.

What s your score . . . brother . . . sister?

Act: The Score

Check yourself. Question you first.

The Score	Overall Range
Soul Brother/Sister #1	0 125
Uncle Tom Tendencies	126 200
Borderline Uncle Tom	201 300
Closet Uncle Tom	301 500
YOUR SCORE	

We Wear the Mask

We wear the mask that grins and lies,
It hides our cheeks and shades our eyes,
This debt we pay to human guile;
With torn and bleeding hearts we smile,
And mouth with myriad subtleties.

Why should the world be over-wise,
In counting all our tears and sighs?
Nay, let them only see us, while
We wear the mask.

We smile, but, O great Christ, our cries
To thee from tortured souls arise.
We sing, but oh the clay is vile
Beneath our feet, and long the mile;
But let the world dream otherwise,
We wear the mask!

*Paul Laurence
Dunbar*

Know.

The Totem

In my innermost vein
I must hide him,
My ancestor with the lightning-scarred,
the stormy skin.
I must hide my guardian animal
Or a scandal will break out. His
is my faithful blood, requiring
my fidelity
To protect me from my naked pride,
And the arrogance of lucky races . . .

*Léopold Sédar
Senghor*

The National Anthem

All please rise for the singing of our national anthem!

Should I rise? Should I sing? I don t give a damn,
but, if I don t, will they wonder why? Sometimes, it s
against my religion. Sometimes, my pride. I fought in
the Revolution. In fact, I was of the first to die. Though
I fought and died, I returned home to slavery. From
the Civil War, my greeting was carpet baggery . My
reward for WWI & II? Lynching, segregation and
discrimination?   Korea, Vietnam, Panama, Desert Storm
and all the rest . . . no jobs, no loans, a second-class
education and sometimes even less. I have toiled for over
350 years to help build this home of the free and brave ,
and yet it takes civil rights movements just to have a
lunch counter where I am welcomed to break bread.
Still, some say, Go back to Africa. My country tears of
thee, when this is my land of liberty, of thee will I sing.
Why don t I sing? You re lucky I even stand!

me

Question #10

When your country's national anthem is played at events, you . . .

   a. Will not stand. (5)
   b. Stand, but will not sing! (6)
   c. Do all of the above, but don t know why?!? (8)
   d. Only if the appropriate person sings! (i.e., Whitney Houston) (2)

And, what s your point:

MLK, (Jr.) Day

Here we go again . . .

A Black man surrounded
a gang wearing hoods and robes
that looked like policemen s clothes, knocking, beating,
kicking the shit out of this man, this Black man
a symbol, and his name is King.
I wanted to burn something down!

Another King, said: I love life. I want to live. Longevity
has its purpose. But, I have seen the promised land.

Oh, what a dream, a place just
for me to be me.

Every day is MLK (Jr.) Day
I am reminded when we get through, what we go
through, we win, peace.

Every day I dream, too, but here we go again.

me

Question #9

Do you still have to ask permission to celebrate the birthday of Martin Luther King, Jr.?

   a. It's not a holiday in your state. (5)
   b. I only celebrate Black History Month. (7)
   c. Hey, it's not a real holiday is it? (8)
   d. He was not like a real American hero! (9)
   e. I just celebrate his birthday!?! (3)

Now, what's your point:

The Million Man March — A Saintly Field of Fireflies

A_{llen} · Still · Angelou · Wilder · Dunham · A_{lexAnder} · Abele · Anderson · Robeson Aaron · Ali · Farrakhan · Mandela · Césaire Baraka · Oprah · Truth · Adam Clayton Asante · Brooke · Banneker · Davis · B_{rown} · Bunche · Fanny Lou · Gaston · Gary · Gray · G_{Andhi} · Bearden · Pippin · Dunbar · Garvey Pele · Russell · Drew · Clausen · Chappie Muhammad · Thorpe · Spalding · Fanon · M_{Arley} · Salessie · Haley · Marshall · Powell · r_{iverA} · Pryor · Gregory · Malcolm Hughes · King · Baldwin · Andy · Whitney Young · Johnson · P_{ushkin} · Jordan Randolph · Sullivan · Mary McCloud Douglass West · Gates · Turner · H. Rap Bobby · Huey P. · Lee Ellington · The Panthers · Carver · Booker T. · Gordy DuBois · Nkrumah · Cosby · Micheaux · B_{elAfonte} Robinson · W_{onder} · Parker · Wilson · Carmichael C_{lArke} · Till · Public Enemy · Toussaint · Bluford · Coltrane Dumas · Shaka · Z_{orA} · Obama . . . and the million man march goes on ad infinitum!

I almost didn t go, cause someone might know, I almost didn t show!

me

Question #8
Your thoughts about the Million Man March . . .

    a. Minister Farrakhan was involved and I didn t want to be associated with someone they say is anti-white. (9)
    b. My goodness, what would people think? I didn t go because I was embarrassed. (7)
    c. Too many niggas in one place! (6)
    d. The March is only about men? (5)
    e. Oh Lord, I want to be in that number! (1)

So, what s your point:

Question #7
Our leaders?
What do you think of Blacks in positions of authority?

    a. No power. The real power is somewhere else! (8)
    b. They only got it because they needed a token! (7)
    c. They gonna mess it up! (9)
    d. They cool . . . or at least, they can be! (2)
    e. I know they had to bust their ass to earn it! (1)
    f. Not qualified! (8)
    g. They not really black . . . they just trying to be white! (9)

Mmmmm, what s your point:

Who is really THE Uncle Tom?

Some people would call Martin Luther King, Jr. an Uncle Tom while others would say he was a prophet. Many called Malcolm X an Uncle Tom but nearly all would cite him as one of our most fiery and inspirational heroes. Was Hattie McDaniel a Tomisine for her portrayal in Gone With The Wind or was she opening doors of opportunity in Hollywood? And what of Jar Jar Binks? Was his characterization the result of unconscious stereotyping? You decide who s the biggest Tom.

me

Question #6

Name your Tom! Search the following list and/or add your own. For anyone you do not know, give yourself one (1) point.

So, what s your point :

Who's the biggest Tom?	yep	naw	who?
Andrew Young			
Bobby Seale			
Booker T. Washington			
Clarence Thomas			
Colin Powell			
Condoleezza Rice			
Dorothy Dandridge			
Julius Erving			
Edward Brooks			
Glenn Loury			
Hattie McDaniels			
Ja Ja Binks			
Latoya Jackson			
M.C. Hammer			
Malcolm X			
Michelle Malkin			
Martin Luther King, Jr.			
Michael Jackson			
Savion Glover			
Michael Steele			
Sidney Poitier			
W.E.B. DuBois			
Will Smith			
Whoopi Goldberg			

Question #5

Ever called someone else an Uncle Tom?

What!!! Well, ummm . . . there was that Sammy Davis, Richard Nixon thing, but that was understandable, wasn t it??? Besides I can t be held accountable for that shit! Anyway, who believes in that crap. Takes one to know one . . .

    a. Naw, naw, hell naw! (2)
    b. True, true, too true!!! (7)

Well, what s your point:

Question #4

Cry,
why!

Why why?

Why . . .

    a. Do I cry because I hate you? (3)
    b. Do I cry because I hate me? (6)
    c. Do I cry because I love you for hating me? (8)

So, what s your point:

The Black White Man (be one!)

I am the white Black man
I am his cousin, his original father
his servant his master his slave
　. . . at anytime, I could kill this motherfucker
　. . . but why bother, he s afraid of his own shadow
　. . . a complete waste of time and mind
Our true bond is beyond solidarity
　　light is one, being is one, mind is one
To know is to be free to be him to be . . .

　　　　　　　　me

Question #3

Don t call me no nigga.

Are you still running around, wondering what to call yourself!?! What do you prefer to be called???

   a. African American (2)
   b. Negro (5)
   c. Black (1)
   d. Colored (7)
   e. Nigga (8)
   f. Afro-Asian-Latino-Irish (6)
   g. Just, a human-being. (4)

Hey, what s your point:

Question #2

"Say it loud . . . ."

   a. Ain t too proud to beg! (3)
   b. I am somebody! (2)
   c. I m Black and I m proud! (1)

And, what s your point:

I toil . . .

You may wish I were never born,
I love my life in-spite of scorn.

At mid-night I was born in this
American segregation
separated souls cast from the same soil
torn between three masters . . . I toil.

You may wish I were never born,
I love my life in-spite of scorn.

In the midst of morning s dew, surrounded I stood
nurtured by saintly fields of fireflies
Martin, Malcolm, and Mandela
were just a few, the chosen ones.

By mid-day I sat learning from new teachers of a darker
pride
dis-covered my heritage torn through and through
dedicated my life to sharing something of it with you
and still, you call me Tom . . . I toil.

You may wish I were never born,
I love my life in-spite of scorn.

Blinded by the glare of setting suns
business became priority, survival pushed prosperity
beyond the realm of dignity, and so I trekked from job to job
a stoic march for the man, and my God: *Now, admit your sins!*

Dream
my devil, seems to come at night
he is an ordinary man
in my dreams. In my dreams
I am afraid, of his light
but, I do not run, I conceal . . . me

 round twilight s bend t ward a brand new mid-night
I submit to life s eternal review
having borne One s cosmic inspirations
yielding gladly, then, capitulation.

Mystic incantations awake
the seeds of whom we are
lain within the rhythms
of my soul.

I recall the love of being just,
what makes you, you and me, me
 till I be One
no doubt God is no doubt. (Selah)

 You may wish I were never born,
I love my life in-spite of scorn . . .

I toil.

me

Confessions of an Uncle Tom . . . I Toil

Question #1

The ultimate goal is?

    a. Wealth (5)
    b. Power (3)
    c. All of the above (5)
    d. Acceptance (8)
    e. Survival (4)
    f. None of this, just love (2)
    g. To be One. (0)

What s your point:

Know.

The Scoring Process . . .

The scores assigned are based on the number of people out of ten who feel that such a response indicates that the respondent is an Uncle Tom. For example: if your response to Question #63 is [c]   she should keep quiet and keep her friends (7)   then 7 out 10 people surveyed (70%) feel that such a response means you are an Uncle Tom or Tomisine.

What s your score . . . brother . . . sister?

Act: The Score

Check Yourself
Question You First

The Score	Overall Range
Soul Brother/Sister #1	0 75
Uncle Tom Tendencies	76 125
Borderline Uncle Tom	126 200
Closet Uncle Tom	201 300
YOUR SCORE	

Confessions of an Uncle Tom ... **I** Toil

Epilogue: A note to me.

The purpose of this work is to resolve an issue that can never be resolved. And, to confront you about decisions you make about you. You are who you are. Recognize your strengths and weaknesses, then, move on. You are an important member of the human race. Do your part.

The point is, God grants to each one(s) own cherished due.

me

Confessions of an Uncle Tom ... **I** Toil

The Final Score

The Score	Overall Range
Soul Brother/Sister #1	0 200
Uncle Tom Tendencies	201 300
Borderline Uncle Tom	301 500
Closet Uncle Tom	501 600
Reference Credit	-
YOUR SCORE	

Appendix (General References) I

References: Earn Credit to Your Race

References & Resources

Earn credit for each of the following that you have read and understand.

1. *A Pictorial History of the Negro in America* by Langston Hughes (3)
2. *A Taste of Power: A Black Woman's Story* by Elaine Brown (3)
3. *A Testament of Hope: The Essential Writings* by Martin Luther King (3)
4. *African American: Voices of Triumph, Leadership* published by Time Life Books (3)
5. *Afrocentricity* by Molefi Asante (5)
6. *American Society and Black Devastation* by Frank Hercules (3) BlackAmericaWeb.com (3)
7. TheRoot.com (3)
8. *The Black Family in Slavery & Freedom* by Herbert George Gutman (3)
9. *Black Mosaic* by Benjamin Quarles (3)
10. *The Black Muslim* by William Banks (3)
11. *The Black Panther Party (Reconsidered)* published by Baltimore Black Classics press (3)
12. *Black Pow-Wow* by Ted Joans (3)
13. *Black Profiles in Courage* by Kareem Abdul-Jabbar (3)
14. *Black Protest in the 60's* by August Meier (3)
15. *Black Resistance, White Law* by Mary Frances Berry (3)
16. *Black Self-Determination: A cultural history of African American Resistance* by (Vincent) V.P. Franklin (3)
17. *Bulletproof Diva: Tales of Race, Sex and Hair* by Lisa Jones (3)
18. *Classic Slave Narratives* by Henry L. Gates (3)
19. *Close to the Bone* by Jake Lamar (3)
20. *Coal to Cream: A Black Man's Journey Beyond Color to an Affirmation of Race* by Eugene Robinson (3)
21. *The Color Complex: The Politics of Skin Color Among African Americans* by Kathy Russell, Midge Wilson, Ph.D. and Ronald Hall (3)
22. *The Envy of the World* by Ellis Cose (3)
23. *Ethical Ambition* by Derrick Bell (3)
24. *From Slavery to Freedom* by John Hope Franklin (3)
25. *Goodbye to Uncle Tom* by J.C. Fumas (3)

26. *High Cotton* by Darryl Pinckney (3)
27. *The Historical and Cultural Atlas of African Americans* by Molefi Asante (3)
28. *King, Malcolm, Baldwin: Three Interviews* by Martin Luther King (3)
29. *The Last Plantation: Color, Conflict and Identity* by Itabari Njeri (3)
30. *Lay My Burden Down: Suicide and the Mental Health Crisis Among African Americans* by Alvin Poussaint, MD and Amy Alexander (3)
31. *Liberation, Imagination, and the Black Panther Party: A New Look at the Panthers and Their Legacy* by Kathleen Cleaver and George Katsiaficas (3)
32. *The Mask of Art* by Clyde Taylor (3)
33. *Modern Black Nationalism from Marcus Garvey to Louis Farrakhan* (3)
34. *New Day in Babylon: The Black Power Movement and American Culture* by William Van DeBerg (3)
35. *Panther* by Melvin Van Peebles (3)
36. *Playing the Race Card: Melodramas of Black and White from Uncle Tom to O.J. Simpson* by Linda Williams (3)
37. *Power and Culture: Essays on the American Working Class* by Herbert George Gutman (3)
38. *Profiles in Black Power* by James Haskins (3)
39. *Protest II: Civil Rights and Black Liberation, the Antiwar Movement— New Directions in Protest* by Miriam Butwin and Pat Pirmantgen (3) *Racism or Attitude? The Ongoing Struggle for Black Liberation and Self-esteem* by James Robinson (3)
40. *Raise, Race, Rays, Raze: Essays Since 1965* by Imamu Amiri Baraka (3)
41. *Salvation: Black People and Love* by Bell Hooks (3)
42. *The Shaping of Black America* by Lerone Bennett (3)
43. *Slave Culture* by Sterling Stuckey (3)
44. *The Soul of Black Folk* by W.E.B. DuBois (5)
45. *Soul on Ice* by Eldridge Cleaver (3)
46. *Tar Baby* by Toni Morrison (3)
47. *Thinking Black: Some of the Nation's Top Journalists Speak Their Minds* Published by Crown Publishers (3)

48. *This Side of Glory* by David Hilliard (3)
49. *To Make Our World Anew: A History of African Americans* published by Oxford Press (3)
50. *Toms, Coons, Mulattoes, Mammies and Bucks* by Donald Bogle (3)
51. *Uncle Tom's Cabin or Life Among the Lowly* by Harriet Beecher Stowe (5)
52. *Uncle Tom's Children* by Richard Wright (3)
53. *Walking on Water: Black American Lives at the Turn of the 21st Century* by Randall Kenan (3)
54. *The Women* by Hilton Als (3)
55. *Women, Race and Class* by Angela Y. Davis (3)

Appendix (Poets) II
Poets Referenced

Poets Referenced

1. Black Bourgeoisie by Imamu Amiri Baraka
2. The Souls of Black Folks by W.E.B. DuBois
3. Totem , Léopold Sédar Senghor
4. To A Dark Girl *Poetry of Black America: Anthology of the 20th Century, The*. Arnold Adoff, ed. (1973) Harper & Row, (l. 9 12) by Gwendolyn B. Bennett
5. Return to my Native Land by Aimé Césaire (1955)
6. We Wear The Mask , by Paul Laurence Dunbar

Appendix (Pictures) III
Picture References

Picture References

1. Uncle Tom s Cabin by Harriet Beecher Stowe, Courtesy of John P. Jewett and Co.
2. Slaves revolt in Virginia. Courtesy of Images of Slavery and Freedom.
3. The African from Uncle Tom s Cabin. Courtesy of Jewett and Co.
4. Illustration from Uncle Tom s Cabin. Courtesy of Jewett and Co.
5. Illustration from the Original Edition of Uncle Tom s Cabin by Harriet Beecher Stowe, Courtesy of John P. Jewett and Co.
6. Smoke Topsy Tobaco: 3 x 5 advertising card (St. Louis: Mound City Bag & Printing Co., c. 1900). Caption: I is so wicked! [Trade Mark.] Spect Massa make it lively if he done cotch dis chile. Mf d by the WELLMAN & DWIRE TOBACCO CO., Quincy, Illinois. Courtesy Fortune Magazine, 1934.
7. Uncle Remus Syrup Dis sho am good . Courtesy of Cracker Barrel Stores.
8. Young Folks Uncle Tom s Cabin by Boylon, Grace Duffie, Courtesy H.M. Caldwell
9. Topsy from Uncle Tom s Cabin Lithograph Courtesy of Courier Lithograph Co.
10. Cartoon Illustrating the loyalty of Uncle Tom, Courtesy of Uncle Tom Images and American Culture.
11. John Brown at Harper s Ferry. Courtesy of Cornell University.
12. Portrait of John Brown, abolitionist. PBS.org.
13. Goodbye Uncle Tom Poster, Addio Zio Tom, from Italian filmmakers, Gualtiero Jacopetti and Franco Prosperi.
14. 1903 Edison Catalogue scene of Uncle Tom s death. Courtesy of UTC films.
15. Uncle Tom s Children by Richard Wright, Courtesy of HarperPerrenial Modern Classics

Picture References

16. Lantern Boy, Courtesy of Images from Jim Crow Museum of Racist Memorabilia at Ferris State University
17. Porcelain Tom Doll, Courtesy of Images from Jim Crow Museum of Racist Memorabilia at Ferris State University
18. Uncle Tom Jew. Courtesy Uncle Tom Images.
19. No to Nigger, Courtesy of The Mawasi Co.
20. We Shall Overcome: The History of Civil Rights Movement as it Happened by Herb Boyd, Courtesy of Sourcebooks, Inc.
21. Niggas with Guns documents Black power movement in Carolina. Courtesy Independent Films and Howard University.
22. March from Selma to Montgomery, Alabama. Courtesy of Civil Rights Museum.
23. Little Rock (AK) Nine and Daisy Bates (back row 2nd from right). Courtesy of NAACP.
24. Malcolm X at 37 years old. Courtesy of Estate of Malcolm X.
25. Nigger, An Autobiography by Dick Gregory. Courtesy of Dick Gregory and Pocket Books.
26. White s only 1960 s sign advocating segregated neighborhoods. Courtesy of AP photos.
27. Vivien Leigh and Hattie McDaniels from Gond with the Wind. Courtesy of MGM.
28. Ad for Nigger Mask. Courtesy of flickr.com.
29. Sundown Towns by James W. Loewen were communities that kept out African Americans (or sometimes Chinese Americans, Jewish Americans, etc.) by force, law, or custom. Courtesy of New Press.
30. 13-Part Series exploring affirmative action controversy. Courtesy of African American Policy Forum.
31. Images from Sundown Towns.
32. Separate facilities prevalent during segregation. Courtesy of NAACP.
33. Racial Inequities discussed by Ira Katznelson. Courtesy of W.W. Norton & Co.
34. Michael Hawthorne s book discussing race. Courtesy of W.W. Norton.

Confessions of an Uncle Tom ... I Toil

35. Promotion courtesy of VH1.
36. Image from Spook Who Sat Beside the Door by Sam Greenlee. Courtesy of United Artists.
37. The Oreo® symbolizing Black Uncle Toms. Courtesy of Nabisco.
38. Banana symbolizing Asian Uncle Toms. Courtesy generic food images.
39. Taco symbolizing Latino Uncle Toms. Courtesy generic food images.
40. Apple symbolizing American Indian Uncle Toms. Courtesy generic food images.
41. Sammy Davis, Jr. endorses Richard Nixon. Courtesy of AP photos.
42. Driving Miss Daisy starring Morgan Freeman as a chauffer. Courtesy of Majestic Films.
43. Illustration of Colin Powell carrying the Republican Party in Rolling Stone Magazine. Courtesy of Rolling Stone.
44. Bling Bling. Courtesy Hip Hop world nomenclature.
45. Mouth grills. Courtesy Gold Teeth.
46. Grill. Courtesy Gold Teeth.
47. Public Enemy, the revolutionary and Black consciousness rap group.
48. Dr. Dre and Snoop Dogg
49. Say It Loud. Black Power Anthem. Courtesy
50. Me
51. Amie Cesaire, poet and author. Courtesy Negritude Poets.
52. Paul L. Dunbar, poet and author. Courtesy Oberlin College Archives.
53. Rosa Parks being booked during the Montgomery Bus Boycott. Courtesy of Mindfully.org.
54. Tommie Smith and John Carlos protest at the 1968 Summer Olympics in Mexico City. Courtesy of ABC Wide World of Sports
55. North Carolina A&T students stage lunch counter during civil rights movement. Courtesy of UPI Telephoto.
56. Buttons of the civil rights movement. Courtesy of crmvet.org.

Picture References

57. Bobby Seale, left, and Huey Newton, co-founders of the Black Panther Party for Self Defense. Courtesy of 1967 AP file photo.
58. SNCC Student Nonviolent Coordinating Committee Logo, Courtesy of SNCC, Inc.
59. Civil Rights Movements: A Photographic History by Steven Kasher and Myrlie Evers Williams. Courtesy of Abbeville Press.
60. Martin Luther King, Jr. and Malcolm X.
61. Titans of the top 100 Black business un America. Courtesy of Black Enterprise Magazine.
62. Through My Eyes: The story of Ruby Bridges, first Black student to attend an all-white school in New Orleans. Courtesy of Scholastic Press.
63. Kenneth L. Chenault, CEO American Express, Inc.
64. William J. O Neil, CEO Merrill Lynch.
65. Richard Parsons, CEO Time Warner, Inc.
66. Barack Obama and Family, 1st Black elected 44th President of the United States of America. Courtesy of The Los Angeles Times.

Please Note: Images may be subject to copyright.

Sankofa

no doubt
God is
no doubt

Encouraged

Because you loved me
I have much achieved.
Had you hated me
I must have failed.
But because you trusted and believed
I would not disappoint you
and so prevail.

Paul Lawrence Dunbar

Confessions of an Uncle Tom . . . I Toil

About the Authors

Michael James

Historical context has been provided by Michael James, a Ph.D. candidate in African and African American Studies at Rutgers University. Mike grew up in an unofficially segregated section of West Philadelphia before moving to an integrated (they were the first) small town in Southern New Jersey. Mike graduated from Trenton State College then served over 10 years in military Special Forces and special intelligence.

Donald O.H. Brown

Donald is publisher of Grio Publishing and Chairman of Grio Foundation, Inc. Donald has served on several boards and taught and lectured at West Chester University and University of Pennsylvania. Donald was born in the officially segregated southern town of Heathsville, VA. The family settled in the unofficially segregated suburb (white city) of Trenton, NJ. Donald graduated from Rutgers College and Columbia University after which he worked at corporations including, IBM and Johnson & Johnson.

www.ingramcontent.com/pod-product-compliance
Lightning Source LLC
Chambersburg PA
CBHW061657040426
42446CB00010B/1788